THIS BOOK E

· · · · · · · · · · · · · · · · · ·

NAME: _____

AGE: _____

I LIVE IN: _____

SOME OF MY FAVORITE THINGS ARE: _____

_____

_____

I'M GOOD AT: _____

_____

MY FAVORITE OUTDOOR ACTIVITY IS: _____

MY FAVORITE PLACE TO GO OUTSIDE IS: _____

IF I WERE AN ANIMAL I'D BE A: _____

IF I WERE A PLANT I'D BE A: _____

SOMEDAY I WANT TO: _____

IN CASE OF AN EMERGENCY, CONTACT: _____

_____

MY MEDICATIONS/ALLERGIES: _____

_____

a GIRL'S GUIDE to the WILD

My Nature Journal

AND

Activity Book

RUBY McCONNELL

illustrations by TERESA GRASSESCHI

little bigfoot
an imprint of sasquatch books
seattle, wa

Contents

HOW TO USE THIS BOOK

This book is a place for you to record your outdoor adventures, favorite places, memories, and observations about how the natural world around you changes with the seasons. It's packed with activities and lists for field identification and planning, and it even has some games for rainy days and long car rides. There are also places for you to record your observations of wildlife, seasonal changes, and the weather, and to practice drawing what you see. So, take it with you on your adventures, and use it at home to dream up more. Go outside, have fun, and go wild!

GIRL'S GUIDE
RULES OF THE WILD

1. Ask permission.

2. Make a plan.

3. Collect the right tools.

4. Keep a positive attitude.

5. Help others.

6. Do no harm.

BASICS

PLACES I'VE BEEN

. . . .

PLACES I WANT TO GO

WHAT TO BRING EVERY SEASON

· ·

Make sure to bring all of these essential items with you every time you go on an outdoor adventure, even if the weather's good or you're staying close to home. Find and circle all the words from the list in the grid. Look for words across, up and down, and diagonally. Watch out, words can run forward and backward! See page 193 for answers.

```
N  C  U  N  A  E  Y  A  K  T  A  T  E  R  B  O  I
E  S  U  N  S  C  R  E  E  N  T  S  P  A  E  S  D
U  P  M  E  T  E  S  G  I  F  I  R  A  O  A  K  F
S  I  R  O  E  G  C  E  E  C  B  F  G  R  N  E  I
G  R  X  A  H  R  O  D  S  N  S  W  E  L  I  O  R
E  Z  F  T  L  U  M  T  F  S  N  T  J  E  E  M  S
A  W  L  I  O  A  P  U  H  Q  A  A  S  R  H  A  T
R  B  A  U  T  N  A  I  O  W  C  L  O  D  V  P  A
P  E  S  C  N  I  S  N  M  E  K  E  G  B  E  Y  I
L  N  H  B  E  P  S  S  N  L  S  I  L  N  O  V  D
O  E  L  A  I  I  L  O  D  A  A  A  W  A  U  E  K
S  B  I  T  A  I  H  I  H  C  N  U  L  Y  Q  S  I
S  U  G  I  M  P  Y  N  J  K  C  G  O  I  G  D  T
F  O  H  W  G  U  I  D  E  B  O  O  K  A  E  M  E
C  A  T  L  T  D  U  T  E  I  N  F  O  C  A  R  D
```

INFOCARD • BLANKET • KNIFE • SNACKS • FIRST AID KIT • COMPASS
SUNSCREEN • BEANIE • GUIDEBOOK • LUNCH • FLASHLIGHT • HAT
SUNGLASSES • WATER • MATCHES • MAP • PHONE

4

BLANKET

MATCHES
strike

NOTEBOOK

WATER BOTTLE

FLASHLIGHT

FIRST AID
+

LUNCH

SNACK

PENCIL

MULTITOOL

INFO CARD

CAMERA

COMPASS + MAP

SUN HAT

SUNSCREEN

PHONE

Tips for Making Observations

- [ ] Use more than one of your senses: look, listen, smell, and touch*
- [ ] Be still and quiet
- [ ] Take your time
- [ ] Notice what isn't there
- [ ] Ask why
- [ ] Look from up close and far away

Tools for Field Exploration

- [ ] Notebook or field journal and pencil
- [ ] Camera
- [ ] Magnifying glass
- [ ] Fish trap viewer (see page 24), butterfly net, or collection jar
- [ ] Binoculars or telescope

Things You Can Do to Protect Nature While You're Outside

- [ ] Stay on the trail
- [ ] Pick up and pack out garbage and litter
- [ ] Reduce noise and light pollution
- [ ] Do no damage
- [ ] Follow posted rules, especially about fire
- [ ] Leave no trace
- [ ] Take nothing but pictures

*Within reason—avoid touching wild animals, and don't touch poisonous plants or plants you don't know.

ABOUT FIELD LOGS
....

Field logs are records of the specific sights, sounds, landscapes, and conditions you experience on your outdoor adventures. Most of what we know about the natural world—what it's like, how it works, who we share it with, and how it's changing—we learned from the careful notes taken by scientists, adventurers, and ordinary people spending time outside.

Each seasonal section has log pages for you to record what you see and do when you're outside, so that you can start making your contribution as a citizen scientist. You'll find field adventure logs; animal, bird, and bug logs; and weather logs in each season. If you would like more logs, feel free to photocopy the log pages or start a separate field notebook.

SAMPLE FIELD ADVENTURE LOG

· ·

Location: William L. Finley National Wildlife Refuge

Date: February 14, 2019

What I Did: We visited the turtle ponds and historic Fletcher House. Walked the trail to the wetland prairie and watched birds from the observation deck. Ate lunch on a hill near the oak forest on the Woodpecker Loop Trail.

Sights, Sounds, and Smells: We saw towhees, Varied Thrushes, and Canada Geese (lots of them). All the trees were covered in lichen and moss—it looked magical in the sun! Found spotted balls by the oak trees. They are called "galls" and are made when wasps lay eggs beneath the bark.

Three Words That Describe My Day:

Cold , Curious , Happy

CONDENSATION

PRECIPITATION

EVAPORATION

RUNOFF

ABOUT WEATHER LOGS

Weather is caused by the rotation of the earth, which causes wind, and the heat from the sun, which causes water to evaporate from the oceans before condensing and falling as rain, hail, or snow over land. Weather is also influenced by masses of cold air from the poles and warm air from the equator meeting and mixing. Regional and local weather is the result of all these things interacting with the features of the landscape, such as lakes, mountains, and plains.

Weather Essentials

TEMPERATURE: A measure of how hot or cold something is. We measure temperature in degrees using a thermometer.

ATMOSPHERIC PRESSURE: The weight of air that presses down on any given place on the earth. We measure atmospheric pressure using a barometer. Increasing pressure means sunny weather; decreasing pressure means impending stormy or wet weather.

PRECIPITATION: Water, in any form, that falls from clouds. We measure precipitation using a rain gauge, in inches or centimeters.

WIND: The movement of air across the earth. Wind speed and direction are measured using a weather vane (direction) and anemometer (speed).

Prediction Tips

Record the weather at home and on your adventures outdoors throughout the seasons. Use your observations to predict the weather hours or days in advance.

TEMPERATURE: The coolest part of the day is right before sunrise, and the hottest part of the day is in late afternoon. Clear skies make for cooler temperatures, while clouds may trap warm air.

PRESSURE: Increasing pressure means sunny weather; decreasing pressure means impending stormy or wet weather.

CLOUDS: High, wispy *cirrus* clouds may mean rain in the next 12 to 24 hours. Tall, lumpy *cumulus* clouds produce summer thunder and lightning storms. Sheets of *stratus* clouds can rise, indicating fairer weather, or lower, indicating rain is on the way.

WIND: Use wind direction and speed to predict where and when new weather will arrive. Since it's not always possible to measure the wind speed outdoors, use observations to estimate instead.

THE *GIRL'S GUIDE* SCALE OF WIND INTENSITY*

MILES PER HOUR	WEATHER NAME	OBSERVATIONS
Less than 1	Still	Smoke and steam rise straight up into the air.
1 to 4	Calm	Smoke and steam drift, but wind socks, vanes, or chimes do not.
4 to 7	Gentle breeze	You can feel the wind on your face. Leaves rustle. Wind socks, vanes, and chimes move.
7 to 12	Strong breeze	Leaves and small twigs are in constant motion. Flags and larger objects move a lot.
12 to 19	Light wind	Dust and loose paper move; small branches sway.
19 to 24	Wind	Small trees and medium branches start to sway; small waves appear on lakes.
24 to 31	Strong wind	Large branches move, the wind starts to make noise, telephone wires sway, and umbrellas are hard to use.
31 to 38	Stormy	Whole trees are in motion, and you have to brace against the wind.
38 to 46	Severe storm	Twigs break from trees, larger objects start to move, and it's difficult to walk. Time to take shelter!

Based on the Beaufort Scale of Wind Intensity

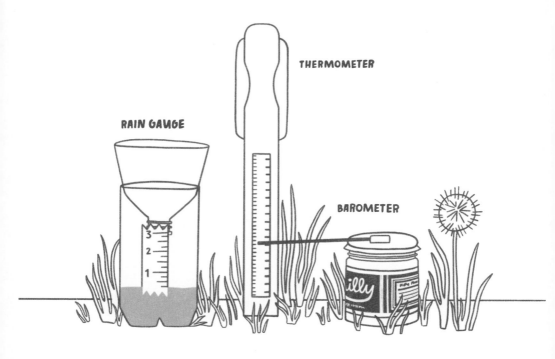

RAIN GAUGE

THERMOMETER

BAROMETER

BUILD YOUR OWN BACKYARD WEATHER STATION

You can start making your own weather observations and forecast at home using this backyard weather station with a thermometer, barometer, and rain gauge. Place or mount it anywhere outside, but try to find a place that is exposed to wind, rain, and sunshine and that you will be able to check regularly.

What You'll Need:

- Hot glue
- Glue gun
- 1 outdoor thermometer
- 1 wood gardening stake
- 1 (6-inch) ruler
- Scissors
- 1 (20-ounce) soda bottle
- ½ cup pebbles or small stones
- Duct tape
- Standard ruler
- Permanent markers
- Water
- 1 balloon
- Craft glue
- 1 glass jar
- 2 rubber bands
- 2 plastic stir sticks or drinking straws
- Clear tape
- Weather log or field journal
- Pencil

What to Do:

1. Choose a location for your station. Look for a place that is open to the weather and not likely to be disturbed.

2. With hot or craft glue, attach your thermometer to one side of the garden stake and the 6-inch ruler to the other, with "0" at the bottom. This will be the stand for your thermometer on one side and the gauge for your barometer on the other.

3. For your rain gauge, cut the top off your 20-ounce bottle and place the stones in the bottom. Invert the cut-off top, put it inside the bottle funnel-end down, and attach it with glue, as in Build Your Own Fish Trap Viewer (see page 24).

4. Cut a strip of duct tape slightly shorter than your bottle and attach it to the outside of the bottle lengthwise, from top to bottom, matching the bottom of the tape with the top of the stones.

5. Using a ruler and permanent markers, draw a line on the tape for each ¼ inch from the bottom to the top of the tape. Label each line.

6. Pour enough water into your rain gauge to just cover the rocks and line up with the base of your tape. This is your "zero" line. You will need to refill it every so often!

7. For your barometer, cut the neck off your balloon and run a thick coating of craft glue around the base of the jar neck.

8. Pull the balloon over the jar until it lies flat, making sure it forms a tight seal with the glue. Secure it with two rubber bands.

9. Tape the two straws together with clear tape to form one long straw.

10. Place a small glob of craft glue in the center of the balloon. Place one end of the straw into the glob so it lays horizontally, and cover with clear tape to hold it in place. This is your barometric needle. When the needle is in front of the 6-inch ruler attached to your stake, you can read increases and decreases in pressure by looking at the position of the straw in front of the ruler.

11. Get the help of an adult to secure your stake in the ground. Place your rain gauge to one side and your barometer to the other, making sure its needle reaches across your ruler.

Record your observations and measurements here in your field journal or in a separate weather log just for your station. Use your *Girl's Guide* scale (see page 11) and compass to record wind speed and direction. Read your barometer; has the needle gone up? Then so has the air pressure. If the straw needle has moved down or is low, the pressure has decreased. Look at the thermometer and read the temperature off the scale. Read the precipitation amount using the ruler along your gauge. Look around at the sky, and note if there are clouds and what kind you think they are. Look for other weather clues, like changes in light, dew, or animal behavior. Compare your measurements to your notes from the previous few days, taking into account what you know about the weather where you are at that time of year. Can you predict what the weather will do?

PSSSSSSST! Remember, when your barometer rises, it means colder weather is coming, while if it falls, warmer air is on the way.

CLOUD TYPES

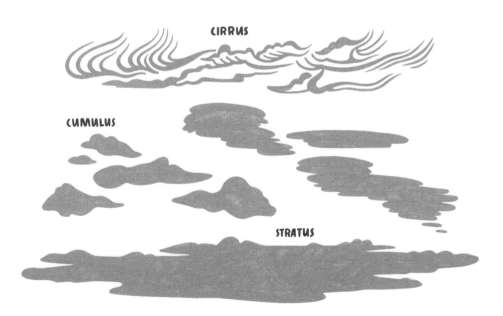

CIRRUS

CUMULUS

STRATUS

SAMPLE WEATHER LOG
. . . .

Location: _Home_   Date: _May 21, 2019_

Temperature: (high)_44 degrees_   (low) _32 degrees_

Barometer: UP or (DOWN)

Wind: (speed)_5 mph_   (direction)_north_

Clouds: (describe)_fog_

Precipitation: (type)_icy rain_   (amount)_1/8 inch_

My forecast: _Tomorrow: cold all day but less foggy in the_

afternoon. No more rain!

SAMPLE WEATHER LOG
. . . .

Location: _Long Tom River_   Date: _July 7, 2019_

Temperature: (high)_78 degrees_   (low) _55 degrees_

Barometer: (UP) or DOWN

Wind: (speed)_none_   (direction)_n/a_

Clouds: (describe) _cumulus_

Precipitation: (type)_light rain_   (amount)_?_

My forecast: _Sunny days ahead!_

ABOUT CRITTER COUNTS

Use the critter count pages to keep track of all the animals, birds, and bugs you see throughout each season, at home and on your adventures. As you add to your lists, think about which critters you see changes with time of day, year, or location. Keep track of when you see the same species multiple times, this will help you determine which are the most common in your area. For an added challenge, set a goal for the number of different species you want to try and see in a particular season or compete with a friend to see who can spot the most wildlife.

Tips for Seeing Wildlife

- Watch in the morning and early evening hours when most animals are active

- Stay quiet

- Choose a location where animals sleep or eat

- Wear colors that help you blend in or hide out of sight

Signs of Life

- Tracks/prints

- Scat (poop)

- Calls/sounds

- Scratches in dirt or on trees

- Pellets and fur balls

- Trails, dens, and burrows

- Broken or chewed vegetation and trees

- Homes: nests, webs, grassy beds, etc.

SAMPLE ANIMAL LOG
· ·

WHAT	WHEN	WHERE
Raccoon	2-18-19	Home
Deer	2-22-19	Ridgeline Trail
Gray Whales	3-15-19	Agate Beach
Frogs	3-17-19	Amazon Park Wetlands

SAMPLE BIRD LOG
. . . .

WHAT	WHEN	WHERE
Chickadees	All February	Home
Flicker	2–8–19	Dorena Reservoir
Towhees and Thrushes	Feb/Mar	School
Bald Eagle	3–5–19	Fern Ridge Reservoir

SAMPLE BUG LOG

. . . .

WHAT	WHEN	WHERE
Moths	Jan/Feb	Front Porch Light
Wasp Nest	2-14-19	Finley Wildlife Refuge
Spider	3-28-19	Bathtub (Yikes!)

WRITE

SIGNS OF SPRING NEAR ME
. . . .

_____

_____

_____

_____

_____

THE WEATHER IN SPRING IS
. . . .

_____

_____

_____

_____

_____

MY FAVORITE THINGS ABOUT SPRING
. . . .

_____

_____

_____

_____

_____

THINGS TO BRING IN SPRING

· ·

- ☐ Rain gear
- ☐ Hat
- ☐ Umbrella
- ☐ Rain boots

- ☐ Wildflower field guide
- ☐ Flower press (or heavy book)
- ☐ Colored pencils and paper
- ☐ Fish Trap Viewer (page 24)

MY IDEAS:

- ☐ _____
- ☐ _____
- ☐ _____
- ☐ _____
- ☐ _____
- ☐ _____
- ☐ _____
- ☐ _____
- ☐ _____
- ☐ _____
- ☐ _____
- ☐ _____

- ☐ _____
- ☐ _____
- ☐ _____
- ☐ _____
- ☐ _____
- ☐ _____
- ☐ _____
- ☐ _____

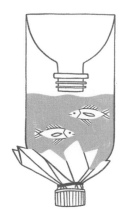

BUILD YOUR OWN FISH TRAP VIEWER

Fish traps make it easy to see even the fastest water critters without causing them harm. Here's how to build your own!

What You'll Need:

- Box Cutter
- 2 (2-liter) bottles
- Ruler
- Rubber cement or hot glue
- Scissors
- Cheesecloth
- Rubber band
- Twine/nylon cord
- Duct tape

What to Do:

1. Cut the top off one of the 2-liter bottles about 4 inches down from the top. Discard the cap and bottom half.

2. Cut the bottom off the second bottle about 4 inches up from the base. Keep the cap but discard the bottom.

3. Run glue along the bottom of the first bottle, and nest it in the second bottle.

4. Run glue around the connection of the two bottles to seal them together, and hold in place for 2 minutes. Set aside until dry, for at least 10 minutes.

5. Cut an approximately 3-inch square of cheesecloth (you may fold it over to double the thickness) and secure it over the mouth of the trap with the rubber band.

6. Tie two loops of twine around the trap, about one-quarter of the way in from each end, making a handle.

7. Secure the handle with a thin strip of duct tape.

8. Submerge the trap in water, allowing it to flow through the cheesecloth. When you catch a fish, secure the bottle cap back over the bottle, so you can lift your viewer out of the water without all the water draining out.

9. To return your fish to the stream, place the trap back in the water before removing the bottle cap and cheesecloth and letting it swim away.

Write about the first time you tried a new outdoor activity (camping, hiking, rafting, etc.). What did you learn?

"In nature nothing exists alone."
—RACHEL CARSON

Do you agree with this famous nature writer? Spend some time outdoors, and write your own observations of interconnectedness.

_____

_____

_____

_____

_____

_____

_____

_____

_____

_____

_____

_____

_____

_____

_____

_____

Try to find, but do not collect, a different thing for each category in the list below (no using the same thing twice). Use the extra lines to add your own categories. Compare what you find in different locations.

LOCATION 1

THREE KINDS OF FLOWERS _____

A NEST _____

A TREE BUD _____

TWO SHADES OF GREEN _____

SOMETHING ROUND _____

SOMETHING SOFT _____

SOMETHING PURPLE _____

SOMETHING THAT SMELLS GOOD _____

SOMETHING THAT MAKES A NOISE _____

SOMETHING WET _____

A BABY ANIMAL _____

A RAINBOW OR CLOUD _____

MY CATEGORIES: _____

_____

LOCATION 2

LOCATION 3

If you could go on an adventure anyplace, right now, where would it be, with whom, and why? What would you see and do?

MY QUESTIONS ABOUT SPRING

. . . .

Example: *Why do some trees leaf out before others?*

_____

_____

_____

_____

_____

_____

_____

_____

_____

_____

_____

_____

_____

Can you answer any of your questions using your own
observations of the season? Try making your best guess,
then research to see if you are right.

SPRING ACTIVITIES

What kinds of sports and activities are popular in spring where you live? Are there activities you want to do? Circle the ones you like to do or want to try, and add your own favorites to the list below.

FISHING

BOULDERING

HIKING

WATERFALL HUNTING

GARDENING

PLANT IDENTIFICATION

BUG COLLECTION

CANOEING (LAKES)

MY FAVORITE THINGS TO DO IN SPRING:

_____   _____

_____   _____

_____   _____

_____   _____

_____   _____

_____   _____

WARM UP!

· · · · · · · · · · · · · · · ·

Draw something familiar—like a mushroom, bird,
or flower—from memory with your eyes closed.

LOCATION: _____ DATE: _____

Write about the first time you tried a new outdoor activity (camping, hiking, rafting, etc.). What did you learn?

SPRING SMELLING

· ·

Find a place outside where you can do a little exploring without
being disturbed or distracted. Spend a few minutes just taking
time to smell (trees, flowers, the ground, the air, etc.). Write about
the things you smell and what they make you think or feel.

_____

_____

_____

_____

_____

_____

_____

_____

_____

_____

_____

_____

_____

_____

Choose a special place to sketch at two different times
of the day, showing how the scene has changed.

TIME:_____

LOCATION: _____ **DATE:** _____

TIME:_____

JACKIE AND THE BEANSTALK

· ·

One morning, Jackie took her _Camel_ to the market
TYPE OF TRANSPORTATION

to buy _Parsley_ for her _cousin_, but she returned with
TYPE OF FOOD   **FAMILY MEMBER**

magic bean seeds from an old man and planted them in the garden.

The next morning, she woke to the sound of _Wind_
SOMETHING NOISY

and looked out her window to see the beanstalks were up to the

clouds! Curious, Jackie climbed up to discover a world with

axes, _urts_, and the biggest house
OBJECT, PLURAL   **TYPE OF BUILDING, PLURAL**

she'd ever seen! So she snuck in through the _kitchen_ window.
ROOM IN HOUSE

It was filled with magic _oboes_ that played
TYPE OF INSTRUMENT, PLURAL

themselves, enormous _Divians_, enchanted
TYPE OF FURNITURE, PLURAL

wheels, and a goose that laid golden eggs! That
DIFFERENT OBJECT, PLURAL

goose looked really sad inside its cage. Suddenly, she heard the

thumping of a giant _Cyote_ shouting, "Fe, fi, fo, fum! I smell
ANIMAL

the ___toe___ of an Englishman! Be he ___gnarly___ or be he

BODY PART   _ADJECTIVE_

___Slippery___, I'll grind his bones to make my ___Carrot___."

DIFFERENT ADJECTIVE   _TYPE OF FOOD_

Jackie ___walked___ out from her hiding

       TYPE OF MOVEMENT, ENDING IN "ED"

place, stuck out her ___liver___, and announced that she was an

                        BODY PART

English _woman_, that _he_ and his big ___Cheek by___ didn't frighten

                                   FACIAL FEATURE

her, and that he had no right to keep a magical goose captive. She

snatched his keys, opened the cage, grabbed the goose, and slid

home to safety, where she released it back to the wild. Every so

often, she still finds a golden egg on her windowsill.

Reminder:

NOUN: a person, place or thing

PLURAL: more than one

VERB: action word

ADJECTIVE: describes a noun

Write a poem about spring in which each line
begins with a different color.

Draw an animal you've seen on (or in) the ground this season.

LOCATION: _____ DATE: _____

SKETCH

Now draw what the world might look like
from that animal's perspective.

LOCATION: _____ DATE: _____

A DAY IN THE LIFE
· ·

Describe how your ground animal spends its day, what kinds of things it does, where it goes, what it eats, and what things it sees.

_____

_____

_____

_____

_____

_____

_____

_____

_____

_____

_____

_____

_____

_____

_____

_____

_____

_____

_____

_____

THE SPRING SKY

·······················

Draw the sky at sunrise or sunset.
Try to capture all the colors you see.

LOCATION: _____ DATE: _____

Imagine you are a seed in the wind.
Describe your journey.

_____

_____

_____

_____

_____

_____

_____

_____

_____

_____

_____

_____

_____

_____

_____

_____

_____

_____

_____

WARM UP!

Draw something complicated, like a field of flowers, a bird, or a blooming tree, using just simple shapes like circles for petals, triangles for beaks, and rectangles for trunks.

LOCATION: _____ DATE: _____

Find four things to draw up close, using a magnifying glass,
hand lens, microscope, or macro lens of a camera.
Include as much detail as you can.

LOCATION: _____   **DATE:** _____

WRITE

My favorite outdoor place in spring is special because . . .

Spring is always filled with color and surprises! Find and circle all the spring-inspired words from the list in the grid. Look for words across, up and down, and diagonally. Watch out, words can run forward and backward! See page 194 for answers.

```
N  P  U  G  W  R  E  A  D  B  F  N  P  E  T  R  T  C  E  R
E  A  B  U  G  S  T  V  A  D  W  E  U  S  N  I  W  I  M  Y
X  L  N  E  F  T  H  L  O  E  U  D  A  S  H  A  A  B  E  I
N  D  A  R  G  E  Z  R  A  I  R  R  A  B  B  I  T  L  O  A
N  U  E  I  A  P  A  I  Y  O  S  A  E  V  J  A  E  S  Q  N
E  B  O  O  I  I  T  E  K  R  I  G  T  N  O  G  R  O  N  D
W  O  P  A  N  Y  N  V  X  S  E  N  R  I  F  I  F  W  L  R
G  T  N  H  B  L  E  B  I  P  F  I  S  H  T  R  A  P  H  A
R  R  A  T  P  N  U  N  O  U  B  O  D  M  E  R  L  I  U  H
O  T  E  L  G  A  S  I  T  W  O  F  V  D  S  A  L  E  S  I
W  E  I  E  G  Z  S  E  L  I  E  A  Y  I  C  M  P  R  R  K
T  R  C  O  N  O  A  G  N  T  A  B  E  A  O  T  E  A  W  E
H  D  U  E  N  L  N  O  Q  O  S  A  J  N  L  W  S  L  S  N
G  O  K  O  I  I  E  C  O  H  E  B  I  O  O  G  D  T  L  L
J  G  A  M  N  T  Z  A  E  A  B  Y  Y  L  R  D  A  R  U  V
T  K  U  N  R  S  N  C  V  E  I  B  F  P  F  I  B  E  G  W
K  I  A  E  B  O  U  L  D  E  R  I  N  G  U  E  O  R  S  E
I  L  C  L  O  Q  V  N  A  N  S  R  I  T  L  X  E  R  L  U
P  I  U  A  F  H  E  O  N  I  O  D  L  N  Y  U  N  E  A  T
S  B  A  O  P  O  E  T  A  G  I  T  S  E  V  N  I  S  D  G
```

RAINBOW • BOULDERING • WATERFALL • RAIN HAT • FISH TRAP • GREEN LEAVES
HIKE • BABY BIRD • FLOWERS • NEW GROWTH • POISON OAK • INVESTIGATE
PLANNING • RABBIT • GARDEN • SMELL • BULBS • SLUGS • BUGS • COLORFUL

HAVE YOU?

. . . .

- ☐ Collected flowers
- ☐ Planted something
- ☐ Listened for baby birds
- ☐ Found your summer gear (hiking sandals, sunglasses, bandanna, etc.)
- ☐ Walked in the rain

- ☐ Checked your bike tires
- ☐ Made summer plans
- ☐ Caught raindrops on your tongue
- ☐ Smelled the rain
- ☐ Practiced wet-weather fire building (with an adult)

MY IDEAS:

- ☐ _____
- ☐ _____
- ☐ _____
- ☐ _____
- ☐ _____
- ☐ _____
- ☐ _____
- ☐ _____
- ☐ _____
- ☐ _____

- ☐ _____
- ☐ _____
- ☐ _____
- ☐ _____
- ☐ _____
- ☐ _____
- ☐ _____
- ☐ _____
- ☐ _____
- ☐ _____

MY BEST SPRING MEMORY

FIELD ADVENTURE LOG
. . . .

Location: _____

Date: _____

What I Did: _____

_____

_____

_____

_____

Sights, Sounds, and Smells: _____

_____

_____

_____

_____

_____

Three Words That Describe My Day:

_____, _____, _____

FIELD ADVENTURE LOG
· ·

Location: _____

Date: _____

What I Did: _____

_____

_____

_____

_____

Sights, Sounds, and Smells: _____

_____

_____

_____

_____

_____

Three Words That Describe My Day:

_____, _____, _____

FIELD ADVENTURE LOG

· ·

Location: _____

Date: _____

What I Did: _____

_____

_____

_____

_____

Sights, Sounds, and Smells: _____

_____

_____

_____

_____

_____

Three Words That Describe My Day:

_____, _____, _____

FIELD ADVENTURE LOG
· ·

Location: _____

Date: _____

What I Did: _____

_____

_____

_____

_____

Sights, Sounds, and Smells: _____

_____

_____

_____

_____

_____

Three Words That Describe My Day:

_____, _____, _____

WEATHER LOG

· ·

Location: _____ Date: _____

Temperature: (high)_____ (low)_____

Barometer: UP or DOWN

Wind: (speed)_____ (direction)_____

Clouds: (describe) _____

Precipitation: (type)_____ (amount)_____

My forecast: _____

_____

DAY 2

WEATHER LOG

· ·

Location: _____ Date: _____

Temperature: (high)_____ (low)_____

Barometer: UP or DOWN

Wind: (speed)_____ (direction)_____

Clouds: (describe) _____

Precipitation: (type)_____ (amount)_____

My forecast: _____

_____

DAY 3   **WEATHER LOG**
. . . .

Location: _____ Date: _____

Temperature: (high)_____ (low)_____

Barometer: UP or DOWN

Wind: (speed)_____ (direction)_____

Clouds: (describe) _____

Precipitation: (type)_____ (amount)_____

My forecast:_____

_____

DAY 4   **WEATHER LOG**
. . . .

Location: _____ Date: _____

Temperature: (high)_____ (low)_____

Barometer: UP or DOWN

Wind: (speed)_____ (direction)_____

Clouds: (describe) _____

Precipitation: (type)_____ (amount)_____

My forecast: _____

_____

WEATHER LOG

· ·

Location: _____ Date: _____

Temperature: (high)_____ (low)_____

Barometer: UP or DOWN

Wind: (speed)_____ (direction)_____

Clouds: (describe) _____

Precipitation: (type)_____ (amount)_____

My forecast:_____

_____

DAY 6

WEATHER LOG

· ·

Location: _____ Date: _____

Temperature: (high)_____ (low)_____

Barometer: UP or DOWN

Wind: (speed)_____ (direction)_____

Clouds: (describe) _____

Precipitation: (type)_____ (amount)_____

My forecast:_____

_____

DAY 7

WEATHER LOG
. . . .

Location: _____ Date: _____

Temperature: (high)_____ (low)_____

Barometer: UP or DOWN

Wind: (speed)_____ (direction)_____

Clouds: (describe) _____

Precipitation: (type)_____ (amount)_____

My forecast:_____

_____

ANIMAL LOG
· ·

WHAT	WHEN	WHERE

BIRD LOG

· · · · · · · · · · · · · · · ·

WHAT	WHEN	WHERE

BUG LOG

· · · · · · · · · · · · · · · ·

WHAT	WHEN	WHERE

SIGNS OF SUMMER NEAR ME

THE WEATHER IN SUMMER IS

MY FAVORITE THINGS ABOUT SUMMER

THINGS TO BRING IN SUMMER

- ☐ Sun hat
- ☐ Sunscreen
- ☐ Extra water
- ☐ Butterfly net
- ☐ Shade umbrella
- ☐ Swimsuit
- ☐ Towel

- ☐ Sandals
- ☐ Sunglasses
- ☐ Inner tubes
- ☐ Magnifying glass
- ☐ Insect field guide
- ☐ Outdoor activity bin
  (see page 66)

MY IDEAS:

- ☐ _____
- ☐ _____
- ☐ _____
- ☐ _____
- ☐ _____
- ☐ _____
- ☐ _____
- ☐ _____
- ☐ _____
- ☐ _____
- ☐ _____

- ☐ _____
- ☐ _____
- ☐ _____
- ☐ _____
- ☐ _____

ASSEMBLE AN OUTDOOR ACTIVITY BIN

Make sure you never get bored by assembling your own activity bin that comes with you whenever you go camping. Below are some suggestions to get you started.

What You'll Need to Make the Bin:

- Large plastic tote
- Permanent markers

Things for Inside:

- Deck of cards
- Yarn and/or cord
- Dice
- Frisbee or panning pan
- Paper and colored pencils (don't forget a sharpener!) or crayons

- Fish trap or water viewer (see Build Your Own Fish Trap Viewer, page 24)
- Sports gear like helmets, bike pumps, goggles, ball pumps, and balls

- Collection boxes, nets, and flower presses
- What else can you add?

  _____

  _____

  _____

What to Do:

1. Gather the contents of your bin.

2. On one end of the box, make a list of all your favorite games to play outside.

3. On the other side of the box, list all the contents.

4. Pack your bin and decorate the two remaining sides with drawings of your favorite animals, plants, or constellations.

Try to find, but do not collect, a different thing for each category in the list below (no using the same thing twice). Use the extra lines to add your own categories. Compare what you find in different locations.

LOCATION 1

SOMETHING SHINY _____

SOMETHING GROWING _____

SOMETHING DRY _____

SOMETHING BROWN _____

A SHADOW _____

SOMETHING FLYING _____

SOMETHING HOT _____

SOMETHING YELLOW _____

SOMETHING INTERESTING _____

TWO DIFFERENT KINDS OF ROCKS 1.

2. _____

AN INSECT _____

MY CATEGORIES: _____ _____

_____ _____

LOCATION 2

LOCATION 3

Summer break can mean more free time to spend with friends.
Write five sentences that start with "Friendship is ..."

MY QUESTIONS ABOUT SUMMER

Example: *What are shooting stars?*

_____

_____

_____

_____

_____

_____

_____

_____

_____

_____

_____

_____

_____

_____

_____

Can you answer any of your questions using your own
observations of the season? Try making your best guess,
then research to see if you are right.

SUMMER ACTIVITIES

· ·

What kinds of sports and activities are popular in summer where you live? Are there activities you want to do? Circle the ones you like to do or want to try, and add your own favorites to the list below.

ROCK COLLECTING   ROCK CLIMBING

SURFING   MOUNTAIN BIKING

WHITE-WATER RAFTING   SWIMMING

MOUNTAIN CLIMBING   HORSEBACK RIDING

LONG-DISTANCE TRIPS

MY FAVORITE THINGS TO DO IN SUMMER:

_____   _____

_____   _____

_____   _____

_____   _____

_____   _____

INVENT YOUR OWN SUMMER GAME

Keep summer fun by making up your own outdoor game, inspired by more familiar games like tag and capture the flag. Try to include as many natural features (rocks, trees, critters, etc.) as you can.

What You Might Need (It's All up to You!):

- Paper and pencil
- Balls
- Flags
- Timers
- Sidewalk chalk
- Imagination!

What to Do:

1. Choose what kind of game you want to play: relay, observation, team game, etc.

2. Choose what the action or goal of the game is: finding, chasing, tagging, collecting.

3. Decide if there are points, time-outs, or other special rules, and write them down.

4. Mark the boundaries or bases with flags or sidewalk chalk or by using landmarks.

5. If you have teams, decide how they will be chosen: by captains, by counting off, etc.

6. Decide how turns will be taken and how the game starts and ends.

7. Gather any needed equipment.

8. Teach your new game to a group of friends or family.

WARM UP!

· · · · · · · · · · · · · · · ·

Pick an outdoor scene or object to sketch, and give
yourself just three minutes to finish.

LOCATION: _____ DATE: _____

"It is the nature of water
to want to be somewhere else."
—MARY OLIVER

How does this famous poet's quote make you feel?

_____

_____

_____

_____

_____

_____

_____

_____

_____

_____

_____

_____

_____

_____

SKETCH

Cut a 4-by-4-inch square out of a piece of regular 8-by-11-inch paper. Use this to "frame" your outdoor view. Draw what you frame.

LOCATION: _____ DATE: _____

SUMMER SEEING

· ·

Spend a few minutes outside really looking closely at
everything around you. Notice shapes, colors, and patterns.
What things are moving or still? How do light and shadow
change your view? Write about the things you see, especially
the things you may have not noticed before.

_____

_____

_____

_____

_____

_____

_____

_____

_____

_____

_____

_____

_____

RAPUNZEL

· · · · · · · · · · · · · · · · ·

One _____ morning, Princess Rapunzel awoke to find
　　　　ADJECTIVE

herself locked in a high tower by an evil _____.
　　　　　　　　　　　　　　　　　　　　　　　MONSTER

Thinking fast, she used a handy mirror to signal for help, bringing

a(n) _____ prince riding a(n) _____ to the base of
　　　ADJECTIVE　　　　　　　　　　　ANIMAL

the tower. "Rapunzel!" he called. "I will save you! Throw down your

mane of _____ hair, and I will climb up it to you!"
　　　　　COLOR

Rapunzel thought this was a(n) _____ idea. She didn't
　　　　　　　　　　　　　　NEGATIVE ADJECTIVE

have a long braid that would reach to the ground, since she had cut

it so it wouldn't get in her way when she was _____.
　　　　　　　　　　　　　　　　　　　　　TYPE OF OUTDOOR SPORT,
　　　　　　　　　　　　　　　　　　　　　ENDING IN "ING"

She didn't see what good it would do to have that _____
　　　　　　　　　　　　　　　　　　　　　　　　NEGATIVE TRAIT

prince climb up the tower—he'd just get stuck up there with her. So

she sent him away. But her signal had also caught the attention of

a friendly and _____ group of _____ that
　　　　　　　POSITIVE ADJECTIVE　　　　　ANIMAL

brought her _____ and _____. She
                  SOMETHING STICKY   **PLANTS**

fashioned a rope and used her climbing skills to rappel down the

tower. She lived happily ever after.

For category reminders, see page 39.

Make up a scary campfire story where the
main character is a girl your age who saves the day.

_____

_____

_____

_____

_____

_____

_____

_____

_____

_____

_____

_____

_____

_____

_____

Draw the biggest animal that you've seen this season.

LOCATION: _____   DATE: _____

SKETCH

Now draw what the world looks like from that animal's perspective.

LOCATION: _____ DATE: _____

A DAY IN THE LIFE

. . . .

Describe how your big animal spends its day, what kinds of things
it does, where it goes, what it eats, and what things it sees.

_____

_____

_____

_____

_____

_____

_____

_____

_____

_____

_____

_____

_____

_____

_____

_____

_____

_____

_____

THE SUMMER SKY
· ·

From a location without a lot of lights blocking your view, sketch the constellations you can see in the nighttime sky, and the Milky Way, the fuzzy band of light that runs across it. The Milky Way is made up of at least a billion stars, one of which is our sun. It is best seen in summer months because the earth is positioned so that we look into the brightest part—the center of our own galaxy!

LOCATION: _____ **DATE:** _____

Write about an outdoor sport you love or an athlete who excites and inspires you. What's the most exciting or challenging part of the sport? How old was the athlete when they started? Do you have sports dreams of your own? (Don't have one? Search world championship videos of your favorite sports.)

Imagine you are a shell in the ocean. Describe your travels.

_____

_____

_____

_____

_____

_____

_____

_____

_____

_____

_____

_____

_____

_____

_____

_____

_____

_____

Write a rhyming poem about an animal you saw this season.

Example: *As I went walking down the road,*
I saw a funny looking toad . . .

_____

_____

_____

_____

_____

_____

_____

_____

_____

_____

_____

_____

_____

_____

_____

_____

_____

_____

WARM UP!

· · · · · · · · · · · · · · · ·

Practice shrinking things down by drawing the same
thing from 2, 10, and 100 feet away.

LOCATION: _____ DATE: _____

Tell (or make up) a story about a time your group
of friends had an outdoor adventure.

_____

_____

_____

_____

_____

_____

_____

_____

_____

_____

_____

_____

_____

_____

_____

_____

_____

_____

SKETCH

Sketch a landscape, focusing on showing how
objects change with distance.

LOCATION: _____ DATE: _____

Hint: The trees farther away from you will look smaller, even if they are the same size in real life.

Summer is jam-packed with fun things to do and curious things to see outdoors. Find and circle all the words from the list in the grid. Look for these summertime words across, up and down, and diagonally. Watch out, words can run forward and backward!
See page 195 for answers.

```
K  S  T  Y  V  A  T  R  T  F  X  Y  T  L  A  U  C  H  E  V
F  I  S  H  T  R  A  P  E  L  T  S  A  C  D  N  A  S  O  N
T  U  A  P  W  T  A  I  N  C  L  A  O  T  A  U  E  O  L  A
H  E  A  T  W  A  V  E  S  B  Z  M  R  E  E  M  R  D  O  N
U  E  G  I  D  B  L  O  W  O  I  L  A  I  O  A  P  O  P  B
N  I  B  I  N  I  U  U  S  G  A  D  E  S  E  U  C  H  O  S
D  G  I  E  F  C  I  T  J  E  M  A  Q  R  U  Y  S  R  K  N
E  T  X  P  G  Y  W  I  T  I  N  U  A  T  I  N  V  T  E  I
R  B  A  L  O  C  V  E  N  E  I  L  E  U  I  G  H  I  M  J
U  C  O  N  O  L  C  N  E  T  R  Y  M  E  Q  E  T  A  E  N
A  D  R  U  L  E  E  D  O  D  L  F  I  O  S  Z  R  L  T  A
S  H  E  H  A  P  U  G  D  T  I  W  L  A  K  E  E  T  E  I
I  L  E  M  O  N  A  D  E  F  A  H  K  Y  O  N  S  A  O  O
O  S  N  R  F  R  I  H  L  U  G  E  Y  O  H  B  A  F  R  E
S  G  E  L  T  E  S  X  I  O  E  K  W  S  Y  T  A  C  S  E
A  A  E  W  L  J  P  E  I  N  T  L  A  O  A  H  E  T  H  W
S  E  N  D  I  G  U  I  D  T  D  B  Y  R  E  E  K  V  O  N
E  A  D  D  E  R  M  G  O  U  A  N  A  O  D  A  N  Z  W  A
O  A  N  T  A  E  R  I  F  T  S  E  R  O  F  D  I  T  E  U
P  E  V  D  A  L  B  V  E  A  O  F  Q  P  U  L  R  Y  R  T
```

THUNDER · CAMP · BUTTERFLY · MILKY WAY · HEAT WAVE · MOSQUITO
SUN HAT · FOREST FIRE · METEOR SHOWER · SANDCASTLE · LAKE
SANDAL · LEMONADE SCAT · BICYCLE · HORSE · PADDLE · FISH TRAP

What is it like in the environment where you live? Compare your environment with one that is very different (desert, forest, mountains, beach, etc.). Which would you rather live in and why?

_____

_____

_____

_____

_____

_____

_____

_____

_____

_____

_____

_____

_____

_____

_____

_____

_____

_____

HAVE YOU?
. . . .

- ☐ Jumped into cold water
- ☐ Smelled dusty earth
- ☐ Lain in the sun
- ☐ Caught a tadpole
- ☐ Looked under a rock
- ☐ Seen a shooting star
- ☐ Flown a kite

- ☐ Slept outside
- ☐ Picnicked
- ☐ Walked barefoot
- ☐ Skipped stones
- ☐ Listened to crickets
- ☐ Sung a song of your own

MY IDEAS:

- ☐ _____
- ☐ _____
- ☐ _____
- ☐ _____
- ☐ _____
- ☐ _____
- ☐ _____
- ☐ _____
- ☐ _____
- ☐ _____
- ☐ _____

- ☐ _____
- ☐ _____
- ☐ _____
- ☐ _____
- ☐ _____
- ☐ _____
- ☐ _____
- ☐ _____
- ☐ _____
- ☐ _____
- ☐ _____

MY BEST SUMMER MEMORY

FIELD ADVENTURE LOG

· ·

Location: _____

Date: _____

What I Did: _____

_____

_____

_____

_____

Sights, Sounds, and Smells: _____

_____

_____

_____

_____

_____

Three Words That Describe My Day:

_____, _____, _____

FIELD ADVENTURE LOG
······································

Location: _____

Date: _____

What I Did: _____
_____
_____
_____
_____

Sights, Sounds, and Smells: _____
_____
_____
_____
_____
_____

Three Words That Describe My Day:

_____, _____, _____

FIELD ADVENTURE LOG

································

Location: _____

Date: _____

What I Did: _____

_____

_____

_____

_____

Sights, Sounds, and Smells: _____

_____

_____

_____

_____

_____

Three Words That Describe My Day:

_____, _____, _____

FIELD ADVENTURE LOG

· ·

Location: _____

Date: _____

What I Did: _____

_____

_____

_____

_____

Sights, Sounds, and Smells: _____

_____

_____

_____

_____

_____

Three Words That Describe My Day:

_____, _____, _____

DAY 1

WEATHER LOG
. . . .

Location: _____ Date: _____

Temperature: (high)_____ (low)_____

Barometer: UP or DOWN

Wind: (speed)_____ (direction)_____

Clouds: (describe) _____

Precipitation: (type)_____ (amount)_____

My forecast: _____

_____

DAY 2

WEATHER LOG
. . . .

Location: _____ Date: _____

Temperature: (high)_____ (low)_____

Barometer: UP or DOWN

Wind: (speed)_____ (direction)_____

Clouds: (describe) _____

Precipitation: (type)_____ (amount)_____

My forecast: _____

_____

DAY 3

WEATHER LOG
. . . .

Location: _____ *Date:* _____

Temperature: (high)_____ (low)_____

Barometer: UP or DOWN

Wind: (speed)_____ (direction)_____

Clouds: (describe) _____

Precipitation: (type)_____ (amount)_____

*My forecast:*_____

_____

DAY 4

WEATHER LOG
. . . .

Location: _____ *Date:* _____

Temperature: (high)_____ (low)_____

Barometer: UP or DOWN

Wind: (speed)_____ (direction)_____

Clouds: (describe) _____

Precipitation: (type)_____ (amount)_____

My forecast: _____

_____

DAY 5

WEATHER LOG

· · · · · · · · · · · · · · · · · · · ·

Location: _____   Date: _____

Temperature: (high)_____   (low)_____

Barometer: UP or DOWN

Wind: (speed)_____   (direction)_____

Clouds: (describe) _____

Precipitation: (type)_____   (amount)_____

My forecast:_____

_____

DAY 6

WEATHER LOG

· · · · · · · · · · · · · · · · · · · ·

Location: _____   Date: _____

Temperature: (high)_____   (low)_____

Barometer: UP or DOWN

Wind: (speed)_____   (direction)_____

Clouds: (describe) _____

Precipitation: (type)_____   (amount)_____

My forecast:_____

_____

WEATHER LOG

Location: _____ Date: _____

Temperature: (high)_____ (low)_____

Barometer: UP or DOWN

Wind: (speed)_____ (direction)_____

Clouds: (describe) _____

Precipitation: (type)_____ (amount)_____

My forecast:_____

_____

ANIMAL LOG
· · · · · · · · · · · · · · · · · · · ·

WHAT	WHEN	WHERE

BIRD LOG

· · · · · · · · · · · · · · · ·

WHAT	WHEN	WHERE

BUG LOG

. . . .

WHAT	WHEN	WHERE

SIGNS OF FALL NEAR ME

THE WEATHER IN FALL IS

MY FAVORITE THINGS ABOUT FALL

THINGS TO BRING IN FALL

· ·

☐ Rain gear

☐ Jacket or warm layer

☐ Collecting basket

☐ Camera

☐ Magnifying glass

☐ Flashlight

☐ Shrub and tree field guide

☐ Miner's pan (see page 111)

☐ Hand trowel (for collecting rocks)

MY IDEAS:

☐ _____

☐ _____

☐ _____

☐ _____

☐ _____

☐ _____

☐ _____

☐ _____

☐ _____

☐ _____

☐ _____

☐ _____

☐ _____

☐ _____

☐ _____

☐ _____

☐ _____

☐ _____

☐ _____

☐ _____

A DAY IN THE LIFE
....

Describe how your aquatic animal spends its day, what kinds of things it does, where it goes, what it eats, and what things it sees.

_____

_____

_____

_____

_____

_____

_____

_____

_____

_____

_____

_____

_____

_____

_____

_____

_____

_____

_____

PAN FOR GOLD (AND OTHER METALS)

Use a shallow, ribbed bowl and water to find, sort, and collect gold and other precious stones from stream and lake beds, just like miners do, hoping to strike it rich! Once you get the hang of panning, you can start bagging and tagging your finds with the help of a geology or panning field guide. There are lots of semiprecious stones and metals that can be found using this technique. Look for books that focus on your area, or ask a local ranger what kinds of rocks are most common.

What You'll Need:

- Panning pan, metal pie pan, or large plastic Frisbee
- Kitchen sieve or sifter
- Magnet
- Plastic bags (for samples)
- Markers

What to Do:

1. Choose a location with lots of loose sediment (sand, silt, and gravel) at the edges of water, like shallow streams, ocean shores, or lakesides.

2. Scoop one or two handfuls of sediment into your pan, and submerge it into the water. Shift the pan gently up and down, letting the lighter bits float away (gold and other metals are dense and will sink to the bottom of the pan).

3. Lift the pan out of the water and gently swirl the remaining sediment and water in a circle, allowing the medium-sized particles to wash out. Repeat this process, adding more water, until most of the sediment is removed. This step is great for finding agates and other interesting nonmetallic stones.

4. Sort the remaining sediment by size using a kitchen sieve or sifter, and separate out iron-bearing minerals, like magnetite, using a magnet. Look in the remaining sediment for fragments and flakes with a shiny, metallic luster—they might be gold!

5. Place your sorted material in a plastic bag. Label it with the date, location, and what kind of rock you think it is.

Write a letter to a younger you. What would you tell
her about being brave?

Dear Me,

Sincerely,

Myself

Try to find, but do not collect, a different thing for each category in the list below (no using the same thing twice). Use the extra lines to add your own categories. Compare what you find in different locations.

LOCATION 1

SOMETHING WITH SPOTS

A MUSHROOM

SOMETHING DECOMPOSING

SOMETHING BROWN

SOMETHING CRISPY

SOMETHING TALL

A NUT OR SEED

SOMETHING ORANGE

SOMETHING MOVING

SOMETHING IN A GROUP

A SPIDER'S WEB

SOMETHING BURIED

A HOLE, HOLLOW, OR BURROW

MY CATEGORIES: _____

_____

LOCATION 2

LOCATION 3

MY QUESTIONS ABOUT FALL

Example: What kinds of birds migrate this time of year?

_____

_____

_____

_____

_____

_____

_____

_____

_____

_____

_____

_____

_____

_____

_____

Can you answer any of your questions using your own
observations of the season? Try making your best guess,
then research to see if you are right.

FALL ACTIVITIES

What kinds of sports and activities are popular in fall where you live? Are there activities you wish you could do? Circle the ones you like to do or want to try, and add your own favorites to the list below.

HIKING FISHING

FORAGING COLLECTING

HUNTING SPELUNKING

GEOCACHING PANNING

CANOEING

MY FAVORITE THINGS TO DO IN FALL:

_____ _____

_____ _____

_____ _____

_____ _____

_____ _____

_____ _____

WARM UP!
· · · · · · · · · · · · · · · ·

Draw an outdoor scene without using distinct lines or shapes,
instead just focusing on fields of color.

LOCATION: _____ **DATE:** _____

"The real and proper question is: why is it beautiful?"
—ANNIE DILLARD

What do you think this quote from this famous writer means?

_____

_____

_____

_____

_____

_____

_____

_____

_____

_____

_____

_____

_____

_____

SKETCH

Choose one thing to sketch from more than one point of
view (front, back, overhead, side, angle, etc.).

Perspective 1

LOCATION: _____ DATE: _____

Perspective 2

RECORD FALL IN A SINGLE TREE

Fall can be a busy time of year, filled with school, activities, and holidays. Slow down and enjoy the season by tracking the progress of a single tree as it changes color and loses its leaves. Try having a friend or family member track their own tree, and see which one of you can guess the date closest to when your tree loses its last leaves!

What You'll Need:

- A deciduous (leaf-losing) tree you can see or visit regularly
- A notebook and pen or pencil
- Colored pencils or markers
- A camera (optional)
- Photo album or staples

What to Do:

1. In early fall, choose a tree you can see or visit regularly to watch, making sure it is the kind of tree that changes color and loses its leaves.

2. Decide how often you will make your observations (daily, weekly, etc.).

3. In your notebook, record the date and what your tree looks like. Draw a picture to go with your description (or take a picture).

4. At the end of fall, compile your pictures into an album, or staple them together at one edge to make a flip book showing how the tree has changed with time. Save it for next year to see how things like weather and age can change how and when a tree loses its leaves.

FALL TASTING

· ·

Find a place outside where you can sit without being disturbed or distracted. Spend a few minutes just breathing with your mouth open (closing your eyes can help!). Write about the "taste" of fall.

_____

_____

_____

_____

_____

_____

_____

_____

_____

_____

_____

_____

_____

_____

_____

_____

_____

_____

Write a poem about a falling leaf using *alliteration* (many words that all begin with the same sound).

*Example: The **F**ading leaves are **F**alling **F**ree . . .*

CINDERELLA
· · · · · · · · · · · · · · · · · · ·

Cinderella and her two stepsisters, _____ and
                                        PLACE NAME

_____, went to the ball. The prince, who was
DIFFERENT PLACE NAME

disappointingly _____ and _____,
                NEGATIVE ADJECTIVE   DIFFERENT NEGATIVE ADJECTIVE

asked her to dance. While dancing, Cinderella noticed two boys

teasing her stepsisters. The prince told her the boys were his

friends Tom _____ Bottom and Peter _____ Top, and
              ADJECTIVE   ADJECTIVE

they had told him her dress was made out of _____
                                            TYPE OF PLANT, PLURAL

by _____, her shoes were made of _____,
   TYPE OF ANIMAL, PLURAL   TYPE OF FOOD

and she was as lazy as a(n) _____. "You can't believe everything
                            OBJECT

you hear, especially if it's gossip from _____
                                         NEGATIVE ADJECTIVE

bullies!" she cried. "Those boys are mean as _____.
                                             DIFFERENT TYPE OF ANIMAL,
                                             PLURAL
I've worked hard for everything I have, while they wouldn't know

hard work if it _____ them on the _____!
                VERB, ENDING IN "ED"   BODY PART

They should leave my sisters alone if they know what's good

for them!"

Just then, the clock struck midnight, reminding Cinderella that

she must leave or her charmed _____ would
                                    MODE OF TRANSPORTATION

turn into a(n) _____. They ran outside, only to find that the
                VEGETABLE

prince's friends had run off with her _____,
                                        SAME MODE OF TRANSPORTATION

her stepsisters hot on their heels, chasing them with magical

_____. "Well, I can give you a ride on my
TYPE OF SPORTS EQUIPMENT, PLURAL

enchanted _____," the prince offered. "No, thanks," Cinderella
           ANIMAL

said, and pulled up her gown to reveal _____ hiking boots.
                                          COLOR

"I always come prepared." And she hiked happily home.

For category reminders, see page 39.

SKETCH

Draw an animal you've seen in the water this season.

LOCATION: _____ DATE: _____

Now draw what the world looks like from
the animal's perspective under the water.

THE FALL SKY
· · · · · · · · · · · · · · · · · · ·

The weather often changes quickly in the fall. Sketch the fall sky at a time that shows a change, like between bands of a storm or just as the wind picks up.

LOCATION: _____ DATE: _____

Write a poem about the animals that you've seen this season and how their behavior has changed from summer. Start each line with either "They used to . . ." or "But now . . ."

WARM UP!
· · · · · · · · · · · · · · · ·

Create an entire drawing without lifting your pencil off the page.

LOCATION: _____ DATE: _____

Capture the motion of an autumn scene (falling leaves, wind, running water) by using lines, squiggles, labels, arrows, etc.

LOCATION: _____ DATE: _____

Fall marks the height of harvest season and the mad dash to get ready for winter. Find and circle all the fall-related words from the list in the grid. Look for words across, up and down, and diagonally. Watch out, words can run forward and backward! See page 196 for answers.

```
Z  A  V  E  I  N  A  W  E  A  R  F  I  P  A  R  C  T  R  O
O  S  D  I  V  O  N  Q  Y  B  G  S  I  O  T  S  F  O  A  M
N  T  Q  A  E  S  H  D  L  C  O  D  E  S  U  P  Y  E  I  E
I  O  R  U  M  N  U  F  T  M  C  G  A  T  H  E  R  G  N  T
D  N  O  U  I  T  G  I  U  A  S  I  L  H  J  I  R  E  B  A
R  E  W  A  X  R  I  N  O  N  B  F  T  A  R  A  N  K  O  N
E  S  R  G  I  L  R  E  S  I  L  U  C  A  T  E  O  G  O  R
O  U  M  A  I  P  H  E  E  L  S  V  X  I  O  E  H  R  T  C
M  I  S  T  Y  E  A  M  L  N  P  T  O  O  D  W  E  B  S  U
S  W  E  E  F  P  U  M  P  K  I  N  Y  A  E  L  R  T  L  I
R  I  N  Q  U  N  F  E  P  A  D  U  T  K  I  T  E  A  S  T
P  R  O  D  L  S  G  V  A  F  E  T  A  P  A  O  E  P  N  O
L  J  D  N  L  I  N  Y  D  E  R  S  F  B  R  D  M  O  D  M
O  L  F  A  M  U  E  G  I  S  W  A  I  G  I  U  T  I  Z  U
E  L  O  D  O  V  E  I  N  I  E  L  W  O  J  D  E  L  H  S
U  R  S  B  O  A  I  N  E  L  B  K  N  A  M  G  E  T  U  H
D  I  T  E  N  I  O  S  E  G  A  D  Z  Y  I  C  Y  G  B  R
Y  T  O  V  T  C  E  S  O  P  M  O  C  E  D  R  O  A  E  O
S  T  U  L  E  P  A  T  A  A  W  T  X  T  F  T  S  H  E  O
I  N  E  A  O  R  F  I  L  J  P  A  E  R  I  A  R  O  L  M
```

**RAIN • PUMPKIN • PUDDLE • MUSHROOM • SPIDERWEB • MIGRATION
LEAF PILE • RAIN BOOTS • SQUIRREL • APPLES • FULL MOON • DECOMPOSE
FISHING • NUTS JUMP • GATHER • MISTY • STONES**

Imagine you are an old tree. Describe what it would be like to stand in one place for so long and the kinds of things you would see.

_____

_____

_____

_____

_____

_____

_____

_____

_____

_____

_____

_____

_____

_____

_____

_____

_____

_____

HAVE YOU?
··················

- ☐ Jumped in a pile of leaves
- ☐ Watched a spider weave its web
- ☐ Visited a pumpkin patch
- ☐ Collected nuts
- ☐ Put away your summer gear
- ☐ Found your warm clothes

- ☐ Jumped in a puddle
- ☐ Gone for a hike
- ☐ Climbed a tree
- ☐ Listened to the rain
- ☐ Seen squirrels bury nuts
- ☐ Skipped stones

MY IDEAS:

- ☐ _____
- ☐ _____
- ☐ _____
- ☐ _____
- ☐ _____
- ☐ _____
- ☐ _____
- ☐ _____
- ☐ _____
- ☐ _____
- ☐ _____

- ☐ _____
- ☐ _____
- ☐ _____
- ☐ _____
- ☐ _____
- ☐ _____
- ☐ _____
- ☐ _____
- ☐ _____
- ☐ _____
- ☐ _____

MY BEST FALL MEMORY

_____

_____

_____

_____

_____

_____

_____

_____

_____

_____

_____

_____

_____

_____

_____

_____

_____

_____

_____

FIELD ADVENTURE LOG

. . . .

Location: _____

Date: _____

What I Did: _____

_____

_____

_____

_____

Sights, Sounds, and Smells: _____

_____

_____

_____

_____

_____

Three Words That Describe My Day:

_____, _____, _____

FIELD ADVENTURE LOG

....

Location: _____

Date: _____

What I Did: _____

_____

_____

_____

_____

Sights, Sounds, and Smells: _____

_____

_____

_____

_____

_____

Three Words That Describe My Day:

_____, _____, _____

FIELD ADVENTURE LOG

· ·

Location: _____

Date: _____

What I Did: _____

_____

_____

_____

_____

Sights, Sounds, and Smells: _____

_____

_____

_____

_____

_____

Three Words That Describe My Day:

_____, _____, _____

FIELD ADVENTURE LOG

....

Location: _____

Date: _____

What I Did: _____

_____

_____

_____

_____

Sights, Sounds, and Smells: _____

_____

_____

_____

_____

_____

Three Words That Describe My Day:

_____, _____, _____

DAY 1

WEATHER LOG
. . . .

Location: _____ Date: _____

Temperature: (high)_____ (low)_____

Barometer: UP or DOWN

Wind: (speed)_____ (direction)_____

Clouds: (describe) _____

Precipitation: (type)_____ (amount)_____

My forecast: _____

_____

DAY 2

WEATHER LOG
. . . .

Location: _____ Date: _____

Temperature: (high)_____ (low)_____

Barometer: UP or DOWN

Wind: (speed)_____ (direction)_____

Clouds: (describe) _____

Precipitation: (type)_____ (amount)_____

My forecast: _____

_____

WEATHER LOG

· ·

Location: _____ Date: _____

Temperature: (high)_____ (low)_____

Barometer: UP or DOWN

Wind: (speed)_____ (direction)_____

Clouds: (describe) _____

Precipitation: (type)_____ (amount)_____

My forecast:_____

_____

WEATHER LOG

· ·

Location: _____ Date: _____

Temperature: (high)_____ (low)_____

Barometer: UP or DOWN

Wind: (speed)_____ (direction)_____

Clouds: (describe) _____

Precipitation: (type)_____ (amount)_____

My forecast: _____

_____

WEATHER LOG

. . . .

Location: _____ Date: _____

Temperature: (high)_____ (low)_____

Barometer: UP or DOWN

Wind: (speed)_____ (direction)_____

Clouds: (describe) _____

Precipitation: (type)_____ (amount)_____

My forecast:_____

_____

DAY 6

WEATHER LOG

. . . .

Location: _____ Date: _____

Temperature: (high)_____ (low)_____

Barometer: UP or DOWN

Wind: (speed)_____ (direction)_____

Clouds: (describe) _____

Precipitation: (type)_____ (amount)_____

My forecast:_____

_____

DAY 7

WEATHER LOG
. . . .

Location: _____ Date: _____

Temperature: *(high)*_____ *(low)*_____

Barometer: UP or DOWN

Wind: *(speed)*_____ *(direction)*_____

Clouds: *(describe)* _____

Precipitation: *(type)*_____ *(amount)*_____

My forecast:_____

_____

ANIMAL LOG
· · · · · · · · · · · · · · · · · · · ·

WHAT	WHEN	WHERE

BIRD LOG

· · · · · · · · · · · · · · · · ·

WHAT	WHEN	WHERE

BUG LOG

. . . .

WHAT	WHEN	WHERE

SIGNS OF WINTER NEAR ME

. . . .

_____

_____

_____

_____

_____

THE WEATHER IN WINTER IS

. . . .

_____

_____

_____

_____

_____

MY FAVORITE THINGS ABOUT WINTER

. . . .

_____

_____

_____

_____

_____

THINGS TO BRING IN WINTER

☐ Gloves

☐ Hat

☐ Scarf or muffler

☐ Extrawarm coat

☐ Sunglasses

☐ A warm drink in a thermos

☐ Extra food

☐ Paper and pencils/crayons to make tree-bark rubbings (see page 171)

☐ Flashlight

☐ Bird field guide

☐ Snow boots or snowshoes

MY IDEAS:

☐ _____

☐ _____

☐ _____

☐ _____

☐ _____

☐ _____

☐ _____

☐ _____

☐ _____

☐ _____

☐ _____

☐ _____

☐ _____

☐ _____

☐ _____

☐ _____

☐ _____

☐ _____

WRITE

Write instructions describing how to do an
outdoor skill you've mastered.

Write five sentences starting with "Someday I want to . . ."

Try to find, but do not collect, a different thing for each category in the list below (no using the same thing twice). Use the extra lines to add your own categories. Compare what you find in different locations.

LOCATION 1

THREE DIFFERENT KINDS OF ROCKS 1.
2.
3. _____

ANIMAL TRACKS _____

SOMETHING CASTING A SHADOW _____

SOMETHING THAT SPARKLES _____

SOMETHING BLACK _____

SOMETHING WHITE _____

SOMETHING EVERGREEN _____

SOMETHING COLD _____

A BIRD _____

MOSS OR LICHEN _____

A ROOT _____

MY CATEGORIES: _____ _____

_____ _____

LOOK FOR SIGNS OF LIFE

Winter has some advantages over the other seasons when it comes to seeing wildlife. While larger mammals might be hibernating, entire flocks and herds of new animals may arrive from colder climates. Other factors, like the lack of leaves and underbrush and the presence of snow, can make spotting tracks, nests, and smaller creatures easier.

What You'll Need:

- Binoculars
- Field notebook and pencil
- (Or nothing but yourself, your patience, and your curiosity!)

What to Do:

1. Stay quiet.

2. Wear colors that help you blend in, or hide out of sight.

3. Choose a location where animals sleep or eat.

4. Watch in the morning and early evening hours, when most animals are active. Look for tree scratches, burrows, nests, webs, tracks, scat, and other signs of life to guide you toward actual animals, birds, and bugs.

5. Record your observations in your field notes for a single outing, or check back over several visits.

MY QUESTIONS ABOUT WINTER
· ·

Example: *What animals hibernate this time of year?*

_____

_____

_____

_____

_____

_____

_____

_____

_____

_____

_____

_____

_____

Can you answer any of your questions using your own
observations of the season? Try making your best guess,
then research to see if you are right.

WINTER ACTIVITIES
· ·

What kinds of sports and activities are popular in winter where you live? Are there activities you want to do? Circle the ones you like to do or want to try, and add your own favorites to the list below.

SLEDDING   ANIMAL TRACKING

SKIING   FORT BUILDING

SNOWBOARDING   STARGAZING

SNOW, MUD, OR SAND SCULPTING   OBSTACLE-COURSE RACING

BIRD-WATCHING   SKATING/BLADING

MY FAVORITE THINGS TO DO IN WINTER:

_____   _____

_____   _____

_____   _____

_____   _____

_____   _____

_____   _____

_____   _____

WARM UP!

. . . .

Make your own connect-the-dots page using a
familiar animal or plant.

LOCATION: Ridge crest   DATE: 12/31/22

"Wildness reminds us what it means to be human . . ."

—TERRY TEMPEST WILLIAMS

What do you think this famous nature writer
means by this? Do you agree?

_____

_____

_____

_____

_____

_____

_____

_____

_____

_____

_____

_____

_____

_____

Create a line drawing of a scene using just black and white.

LOCATION: _____   DATE: _____

WINTER FEELING

· ·

Find a place outside where there are lots of things to touch. Spend
a few minutes just reaching out and feeling the things around you
(closing your eyes can help!). Write about the things you feel or
what new things you notice.

_____

_____

_____

_____

_____

_____

_____

_____

_____

_____

_____

_____

_____

_____

_____

_____

Make up a new fairy tale or fable using your favorite
animal as the main character.

_____

_____

_____

_____

_____

_____

_____

_____

_____

_____

_____

_____

_____

_____

_____

_____

_____

_____

_____

THE PRINCESS AND THE _Pencil_
.... SMALL OBJECT

Once there was a prince who wanted to marry a princess. Not just any princess, though; he wanted a real princess, one that, he thought, would be smart and dainty and delicate. He searched _Up_ and _down_ for a young noblewoman and found
DIRECTION   DIRECTION

many who were _Kindness_ and _honesty_,
POSITIVE TRAIT   DIFFERENT POSITIVE TRAIT

but none that were dainty and delicate too. Some were even _Walking door_ or _greedy_, but he was looking for the one
SILLY TRAIT   NEGATIVE TRAIT

that was "perfect," so he rejected them all. Then, one dark and _Stormy_ night, a girl appeared at the castle door. She
TYPE OF WEATHER

was _Kind_ and covered in rain and mud. "Hello!"
SAME POSITIVE TRAIT

she said. "Sorry to intrude, but the weather is awful, and my _automobile_ broke down. Will you let a fellow
MODE OF TRANSPORTATION

noblewoman stay the night? You see, I'm a princess on a great

164

adventure to **Paris** " The prince let her in, but neither he nor his

PLACE

Blue-haired mother believed that she was a princess. She seemed

COLOR

too tough. So that night, they made her a bed out of mattresses

stuffed with **Cat** fur and placed a single **Pencil** under

MAMMAL   SMALL OBJECT

the pile. In the morning, they asked her how she slept. "Great!"

she replied. "The bed was so soft." The prince turned **green**, and

COLOR

his face **jumped** . "I knew it!" he cried. "You

TYPE OF ACTION ENDING IN "ED"

aren't a real princess if you can sleep on a bed with a **pencil**

SAME OBJECT

in it!" Just as he was getting ready to toss her out on her **foot**,

BODY PART

a tiara fell from her pack. "See?!" she said. "You **chair**!

OBJECT

Real princesses aren't delicate **daisys** or fragile

TYPE OF FLOWER, PLURAL

televisions ! And we aren't kept awake by

TYPE OF ELECTRONIC DEVICE, PLURAL

lumpy beds!" She stormed out and finished her adventure on foot,

sleeping on the bare ground the whole way. The prince never found

a perfect princess; they don't exist!

For category reminders, see page 39.

Draw an animal you've seen someplace up high this season.

LOCATION: _____ DATE: _____

Now draw what the world might look like from that
animal's overhead perspective.

A DAY IN THE LIFE
· ·

Describe how your "high places" animal spends its day, what kinds
of things it does, where it goes, what it eats, and what things it sees.

_____

_____

_____

_____

_____

_____

_____

_____

_____

_____

_____

_____

_____

_____

_____

_____

_____

Imagine you are a shooting star.
Describe your journey to Earth.

THE WINTER SKY
. . . .

Draw the sky on a cloudy day using as many shades of gray as you can.

LOCATION: _____ DATE: _____

MAKE WINTER TREE-BARK RUBBINGS

Winter, when the trees are bare, is the perfect time to learn how to identify trees based on their bark patterns. A fun way to capture the details is by making bark rubbings—a printed imprint of the bark's surface. You can use a regular pencil for identification purposes or experiment with using colored pencils and blending colors and textures from several trees to make a mosaic or collage art piece.

What You'll Need:

- A tree
- Semitransparent paper (like printer paper)
- Pencil, colored pencils, or crayons
- Masking tape (optional)

What to Do:

1. Find a tree that you think is interesting.

2. Hold the piece of paper with one hand or affix it with masking tape to the trunk of the tree.

3. Use your pencil or crayon to gently rub across the paper until you can see the underlying texture. Repeat for a darker image.

Write a riddle (or two or three!) describing an animal by how it stays warm and well in winter.

Example: *What's big and fat and fast asleep? (A bear.)*

_____

_____

_____

_____

_____

_____

_____

_____

_____

_____

_____

_____

_____

_____

_____

_____

_____

WARM UP!

· · · · · · · · · · · · · · · · ·

Sketch one small thing, like a nut or stone,
exactly the size it is in the real world.

LOCATION: _____ **DATE:** _____

Create a scene by drawing the things that aren't there,
like the spaces between trees, valleys and depressions,
and shadows rather than objects.

LOCATION: _____ **DATE:** _____

Winter means colder temperatures and shorter days, regardless of where you live. Find and circle all the wintery words in the grid. Look for words across, up and down, and diagonally. Watch out, words can run forward and backward! See page 197 for answers.

```
E  E  D  L  I  R  E  Q  H  N  N  O  I  B  E  G  T  A  I  N
N  F  O  C  I  S  A  S  I  Z  E  S  R  H  A  F  L  B  E  I
P  I  V  S  E  O  M  E  T  L  S  C  P  I  G  H  T  N  O  X
P  A  G  Y  N  I  U  A  R  S  T  O  O  B  J  N  O  A  A  T
U  O  Y  D  T  O  N  E  A  T  C  W  O  E  A  C  E  R  L  T
M  I  D  T  N  E  W  U  O  R  U  D  K  R  E  O  V  E  D  W
N  Z  E  O  I  G  R  F  C  I  E  F  A  N  U  S  E  D  R  R
O  N  L  A  U  O  N  O  L  A  I  S  I  A  I  E  D  O  E  U
S  K  I  I  N  G  T  M  L  A  W  P  E  T  I  G  N  I  A  O
G  L  T  E  R  W  S  E  T  R  K  S  L  E  D  A  S  C  M  T
B  I  F  H  X  A  E  V  B  O  V  E  R  I  P  N  I  E  P  I
R  P  W  D  N  A  N  R  H  E  B  E  Q  C  O  C  O  A  G  T
A  T  E  T  L  U  S  K  N  S  I  Y  J  I  S  A  E  T  Y  O
O  H  R  Z  O  E  D  E  N  A  K  N  L  C  I  J  O  E  B  W
P  O  O  Y  N  E  R  O  Q  O  V  C  S  L  I  D  E  W  I  F
F  E  A  X  F  L  I  A  D  I  T  Y  A  E  V  I  R  C  L  N
R  S  N  U  K  R  B  U  H  L  M  C  E  R  E  G  S  A  E  R
O  B  A  R  O  N  D  G  E  D  S  T  A  R  T  E  T  I  N  U
S  O  D  I  E  S  O  A  D  O  U  G  P  I  S  A  N  O  T  I
T  E  I  M  G  T  E  V  E  R  G  R  E  E  N  U  C  L  O  S
```

SNOWFLAKE · COCOA · FROST · ORION'S BELT · HIBERNATE
TRACKS · SLED · ICICLE · PINECONE · BOOTS · MITTENS · SKIING
FORT · TWIG · BIRD'S NEST · SLIDE · EVERGREEN · DREAM

HAVE YOU?

. . . .

- ☐ Caught a snowflake and/or hail on your tongue
- ☐ Thrown a snowball
- ☐ Tied a knot
- ☐ Made a tree-bark rubbing (see page 171)
- ☐ Listened for owls at night

- ☐ Snapped twigs
- ☐ Counted tree rings
- ☐ Built a fort
- ☐ Stargazed
- ☐ Smelled pine needles
- ☐ Seen your breath
- ☐ Spotted a new bird

MY IDEAS:

- ☐ _____
- ☐ _____
- ☐ _____
- ☐ _____
- ☐ _____
- ☐ _____
- ☐ _____
- ☐ _____
- ☐ _____
- ☐ _____
- ☐ _____

- ☐ _____
- ☐ _____
- ☐ _____
- ☐ _____
- ☐ _____
- ☐ _____
- ☐ _____
- ☐ _____
- ☐ _____
- ☐ _____
- ☐ _____

MY BEST WINTER MEMORY

_____

_____

_____

_____

_____

_____

_____

_____

_____

_____

FIELD ADVENTURE LOG

· ·

Location: _____

Date: _____

What I Did: _____

_____

_____

_____

_____

Sights, Sounds, and Smells: _____

_____

_____

_____

_____

_____

Three Words That Describe My Day:

_____, _____, _____

FIELD ADVENTURE LOG
....

Location: _____

Date: _____

What I Did: _____
_____
_____
_____
_____

Sights, Sounds, and Smells: _____
_____
_____
_____
_____
_____

Three Words That Describe My Day:

_____, _____, _____

FIELD ADVENTURE LOG
. . . .

Location: _____

Date: _____

What I Did: _____

_____

_____

_____

_____

Sights, Sounds, and Smells: _____

_____

_____

_____

_____

_____

Three Words That Describe My Day:

_____, _____, _____

FIELD ADVENTURE LOG
· ·

Location: _____

Date: _____

What I Did: _____

_____

_____

_____

_____

Sights, Sounds, and Smells: _____

_____

_____

_____

_____

_____

Three Words That Describe My Day:

_____, _____, _____

WEATHER LOG
· ·

Location: _____ Date: _____

Temperature: (high)_____ (low)_____

Barometer: UP or DOWN

Wind: (speed)_____ (direction)_____

Clouds: (describe) _____

Precipitation: (type)_____ (amount)_____

My forecast: _____

_____

DAY 2

WEATHER LOG
· ·

Location: _____ Date: _____

Temperature: (high)_____ (low)_____

Barometer: UP or DOWN

Wind: (speed)_____ (direction)_____

Clouds: (describe) _____

Precipitation: (type)_____ (amount)_____

My forecast: _____

_____

WEATHER LOG

· ·

Location: _____   Date: _____

Temperature: (high)_____   (low)_____

Barometer: UP or DOWN

Wind: (speed)_____   (direction)_____

Clouds: (describe) _____

Precipitation: (type)_____   (amount)_____

My forecast:_____

_____

DAY 4

WEATHER LOG

· ·

Location: _____   Date: _____

Temperature: (high)_____   (low)_____

Barometer: UP or DOWN

Wind: (speed)_____   (direction)_____

Clouds: (describe) _____

Precipitation: (type)_____   (amount)_____

My forecast: _____

_____

DAY 5

WEATHER LOG
· ·

Location: _____ Date: _____

Temperature: *(high)*_____ *(low)*_____

Barometer: UP or DOWN

Wind: *(speed)*_____ *(direction)*_____

Clouds: *(describe)* _____

Precipitation: *(type)*_____ *(amount)*_____

My forecast:_____

_____

DAY 6

WEATHER LOG
· ·

Location: _____ Date: _____

Temperature: *(high)*_____ *(low)*_____

Barometer: UP or DOWN

Wind: *(speed)*_____ *(direction)*_____

Clouds: *(describe)* _____

Precipitation: *(type)*_____ *(amount)*_____

My forecast:_____

_____

WEATHER LOG

· ·

Location: _____ *Date:* _____

Temperature: *(high)* _____ *(low)* _____

Barometer: UP or DOWN

Wind: *(speed)* _____ *(direction)* _____

Clouds: *(describe)* _____

Precipitation: *(type)* _____ *(amount)* _____

My forecast: _____

_____

ANIMAL LOG

. . . .

WHAT	WHEN	WHERE

BIRD LOG

· · · · · · · · · · · · · · · · ·

WHAT	WHEN	WHERE

BUG LOG
· · · · · · · · · · · · · · · ·

WHAT	WHEN	WHERE

MY YEAR

· · · · · · · · · · · · · · ·

My Favorite Season This Year: _____

What Made It Special:_____

_____

_____

_____

_____

Favorite Things I Did This Year:_____

_____

_____

_____

Favorite Places I Went This Year:_____

_____

_____

_____

_____

NEXT YEAR
· · · · · · · · · · · · · · · · ·

Things I'm Looking Forward to Next Year:

_____

_____

_____

_____

Places I Want to Go Next Year: _____

_____

_____

_____

_____

Things I Want to Try Next Year: _____

_____

_____

_____

_____

MY FAVORITE THING THIS YEAR

Draw a picture of your favorite place you visited or the
most special thing you saw this year.

LOCATION: _____ DATE: _____

WORD SEARCH ANSWER KEYS

BASICS (page 4)

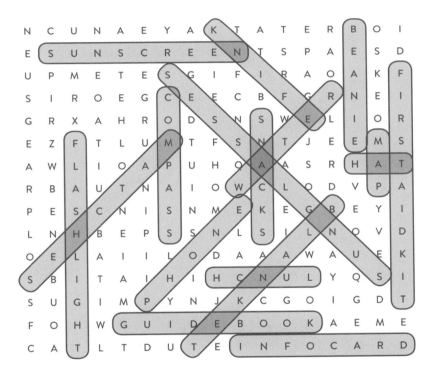

SPRING (page 49)

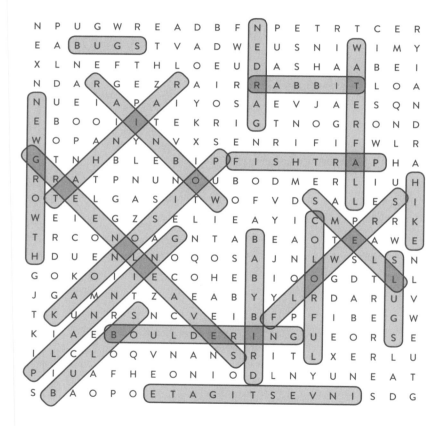

SUMMER (page 92)

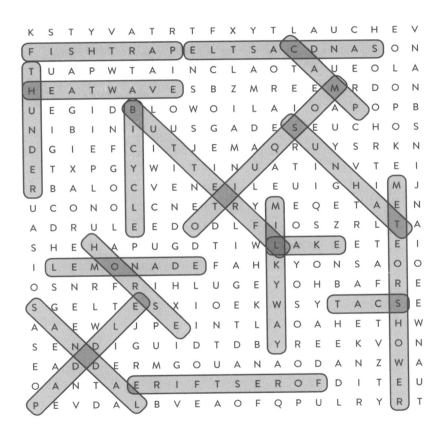

K S T Y V A T R T F X Y T L A U C H E V
F I S H T R A P E L T S A C D N A S O N
T U A P W T A I N C L A O T A U E O L A
H E A T W A V E S B Z M R E E M R D O N
U E G I D B L O W O I L A I O A P O P B
N I B I N I U U S G A D E S E U C H O S
D G I E F C I T J E M A Q R U Y S R K N
E T X P G Y W I T I N U A T I N V T E I
R B A L O C V E N E I L E U I G H I M J
U C O N O L C N E T R Y M E Q E T A E N
A D R U L E E D O D L F I O S Z R L T A
S H E H A P U G D T I W L A K E E T E I
I L E M O N A D E F A H K Y O N S A O O
O S N R F R I H L U G E Y O H B A F R E
S G E L T E S X I O E K W S Y T A C S E
A A E W L J P E I N T L A O A H E T H W
S E N D I G U I D T D B Y R E E K V O N
E A D D E R M G O U A N A O D A N Z W A
O A N T A E R I F T S E R O F D I T E U
P E V D A L B V E A O F Q P U L R Y R T

195

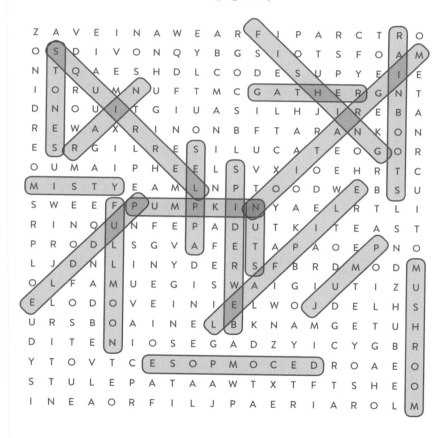

Z A V E I N A W E A R F I P A R C T R O
O S D I V O N Q Y B G S I O T S F O A M
N T Q A E S H D L C O D E S U P Y E I E
I O R U M N U F T M C G A T H E R G N T
D N O U I T G I U A S I L H J I R E B A
R E W A X R I N O N B F T A R A N K O R
E S R G I L R E S I L U C A T E O G O R
O U M A I P H E E L S V X I O E H R T C
M I S T Y E A M L N P T O O D W E B S U
S W E E F P U M P K I N Y A E L R T L I
R I N Q U N F E P A D U T K I T E A S T
P R O D L S G V A F E T A P A O E P N O
L J D N L I N Y D E R S F B R D M O D U
O L F A M U E G I S W A I G I U T I Z S
E L O D O V E I N I E L W O J D E L H H
U R S B O A I N E L B K N A M G E T U R
D I T E N I O S E G A D Z Y I C Y G B O
Y T O V T C E S O P M O C E D R O A E O
S T U L E P A T A A W T X T F T S H E M
I N E A O R F I L J P A E R I A R O L M

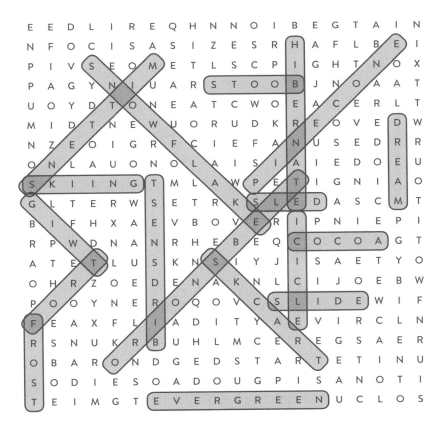

ABOUT THE AUTHOR

RUBY McCONNELL is a writer, geologist, and environmental advocate. She is a proud daughter of Oregon country. You can almost always find her in the woods. Follow her on Twitter and Instagram @RubyGoneWild and at RubyMcConnell.com.